The LORD looks down

from heaven

and sees every person.

From his throne he watches

all who live on earth.

He has made their hearts

and understands

everything they do.

—Psalm 33:13-15 NCV

PRESENTED TO:

BY:

RON LUCE

GUARD YOUR HEART

COUNTRYMAN®

NASHVILLE, TENNESSEE

Published in association with Yates & Yates, LLP, Attorneys and Counselors, Orange, California.

www.thomasnelson.com | www.jcountryman.com

www.teenmania.com | www.acquirethefire.com

Designed by Lookout Design Group, Inc., Minneapolis, Minnesota

Project Editor: Kathy Baker

ISBN: 1-4041-0185-3 hardcover
ISBN: 1-4041-0190-X softcover

Printed and bound in the United States of America

TABLE OF CONTENTS

Good sense will

protect you;

understanding

will guard you.

—Proverbs 2:11 NCV

INTROD

INTRODUCTION

I am in the heart surgery business, a cardiologist, but I'm not a medical doctor. Instead, I specialize in watching hearts change right in front of my eyes. The kind of heart surgery that I see is something no surgeon can perform. On a recent airplane trip, I sat next to a doctor who specializes in heart surgery, and he was interested to hear how although we use the same words, what we do is very different.

"Get rid of all the sins you have done, and get for yourselves a new heart and a new way of thinking."

—Ezekiel 18:31 NCV

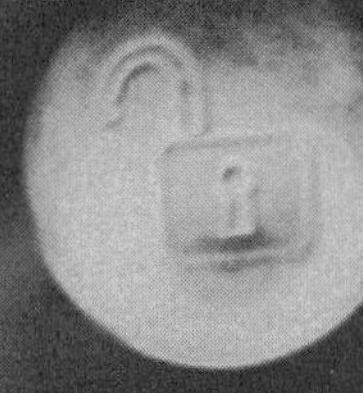

Surgeons can do amazing feats, such as actually replacing someone's heart with a self-contained artificial heart; God, however, has been planting new hearts in people for thousands of years. He is in the heart-changing business. What a tragedy it would be to see a person get a new physical heart and yet still be broken and desperate because they don't have a new heart from God. The new heart that God wants to give each of us cannot come from any human surgeon. I personally have seen hundreds of thousands of hearts change weekend after weekend as I stand in front of teenagers and adults all across this land. I see them bring their broken hearts and lives to Jesus, and I've witnessed the miracle of new hearts beating as they commit their lives to Him.

This miracle is difficult to describe with human words. It sounds like a bunch of Christian jargon until it happens to you. Many people who have been in church for years have heard stories of this "changed heart," but have never had it happen to them, ever. I have seen the hopelessness of kids who have grown up in homes without a mom or a dad or anyone to deeply care about them. They feel like no one loves them, but then their countenances change when the God of the universe comes to live inside them, breathes life into their dead hearts, and gives them all a new start. So many times I have seen a life full of pain and brokenness washed away in a moment as the love of God is poured into

Create in me a pure

heart, God, and make

my spirit right again

—Psalm 51:10 NCV

the heart and soul of a young seeker who commits to live for Christ.

The heart change that I specialize in doesn't just prolong life on earth; it gives each recipient eternal life. It's not about making life longer; it actually changes the quality of life. Someone might receive a new artificial heart on earth to be able to live longer, but that doesn't mean the joy of their life is any stronger or better. However, when God breathes life into a dead heart, He gives meaning, purpose, and a full, abundant life.

I invite you to join me on a journey. This journey will take us to the deepest part of who we are as humans. We are going to dissect the miracle that happens when God comes to live on the inside of us. We are going to find the essential ingredient for living life to the fullest as God intended it to be lived—out of a heart that is full of life from heaven. Together we will explore the influences from our world that corrupt hearts and destroy lives, and we will be empowered to see through the confusion that longs to rob us all of real life. Finally, we will be equipped to make sure the heart-killers, those things that give us the heart disease of the soul, are prevented from destroying our lives because we have found God's wisdom on how we each can guard our hearts.

CHAPTER

A PLACE CALLED DESIRE

Inside every one of us there is a place called desire. This non-physical place called desire has a magnetic pull on our mind, our will, and our emotions. It has the power to push, sway, and drive us to do things that we aren't sure we really want to do. Desire actually rules our lives. Whatever governs the place of desire also rules what we do with our activities, with our bodies, with our minds, and with our time. For instance, imagine you are riding a horse away from

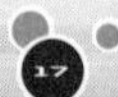

the barn and into a far field. As soon as you let go of the bridle, the horse turns and runs as fast as it can back to the barn where it knows it will get shelter and food. In us, that place called desire carries us all the way back to the barn—the place that we really want to go.

Sometimes this place called desire reveals some ugly truths about us because it really uncovers our true desires. You might have heard a parent say something to their child after promising to be at an important ball game, "I didn't mean to miss your ballgame . . . I really wanted to be there." As the dejected child hears these words he looks to the ground because he has heard them so many times. In his heart

Do you know where your

fights and arguments

come from? They come

from the selfish desires

that war within you.

—James 4:1 NCV

the child says, "Yeah right, you would have been here if you really wanted to." Sometimes unavoidable emergencies do get in the way of a parent keeping a promise, but the fact is that if it happens repeatedly it shows that the parent has more of a desire to succeed at work than to be with their kids and their activities.

The place of desire is like the county seat. In any county there is one designated town. That town has authority over all the rest of the county. The courthouse is there, the judge is there, and the sheriff's office is there, so any major crimes committed in the country are processed there. It is the "muscle" for enforcing the law. The county seat exercises authority and control over the entire county. This place called desire is the county seat of each person's life. It exercises authority control over us whether we acknowledge it or not. Phrases like, "I really didn't mean to hurt your feelings," oftentimes mask that a person really did desire to hurt someone else to give payback for something. Others will say, "I didn't want to do such and such," but that is the problem; they are afraid or ashamed to admit that they really did want to do that thing, and maybe even ashamed to admit it to themselves.

People make bad decisions about their lives and feel broken, hurt, horribly embarrassed, and dejected because they have let wrong things dominate their place of

Doing right brings

freedom to honest people,

but those who are not

trustworthy will be caught

by their own desires.

—Proverbs 11:6 NCV

desire. Desire will either take you to great success or horrible failures in your family life, professional life, moral life, and your spiritual life. Where is that place called desire? Where can you find it so you can put your finger on it? That is exactly what this book is about. That place called desire is your heart, because what dominates your heart is what you truly desire and end up doing. As we set our desires in motion and in the right direction, and as we give them the focus they were meant to have from the beginning of time, we are absolutely guaranteed that where we end up in life and in eternity will be the very best because there will be no foreign forces controlling our hearts.

CHAPTER

WHAT IS THE HEART?

You find yourself in a tough situation: some of your friends want you to do one thing and others want you to another. It is not a simple matter; it is a life or death issue. The decision you make could affect the rest of your life. It could be what college you attend, who you marry, what you major in, or what job you take. In asking advice from a trusted friend, counselor, or parent, you hear these

The heart of the wise

leads to right,

but the heart of a fool

leads to wrong.

—Ecclesiastes 10:2 NCV

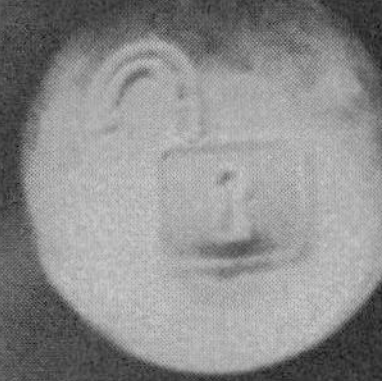

words, "Down in your heart of hearts you know what the right thing is, and I am sure you will make the right decision."

Where is your heart of hearts? How does your heart of hearts know what the right thing is? Someone may ask, "What is your heart telling you?" How do you know what your heart is telling you? Where is that heart? Where is that voice coming from that supposedly comes from your heart?

These questions are hard to answer, but we know that they are valid. Our heart is like a conscience. We know it is real, but we can't see it. It is like love; you know it is a real energy even though you

can't actually see it floating through the air. Your heart is a real part of you that you can't see with your eyes. So what is it?

The heart is actually one of the distinctive features that sets us apart from every other species in the world. It is a sponge that soaks up every experience, every thought, and everything we have ever been taught. It absorbs everything and then, as we are squeezed, what comes out of that sponge directs our life.

Think of all the experiences you have had—good ones, exciting ones, and bad ones that have hurt you. Think of all the things you have seen, read in text books, and learned from the school of life.

Think of every emotion you have ever had and every dream you have ever dreamed. All of those things have been absorbed into your inner being just as a sponge would soak up water. The sum total of all those things helps to guide the decisions you make, determine what you really desire, and point you in what direction you go. Those are the things that make you feel bad or feel guilty when you do something wrong because you know it is not what you should have done.

A dog doesn't feel bad when he steals another dog's bone, because a dog doesn't have a heart, an emotional and mental center that drives him on. A lioness

doesn't feel bad when she kills an antelope to eat it. She doesn't sense that she has committed murder because she doesn't have a moral conscience, nor does she have a heart. God made you and me in His image, and this makes us different from every other creature on earth. The heart is what the Tin Man in *The Wizard of Oz* cried out for. The heart determines the essence of our lives.

Your heart is the deepest part of you. It is the real you. It is the core of who you are. You might have said something like, "From the bottom of my heart I really want to . . ." which indicates that the deepest part of you really wants to do such and such. You might have heard somebody ask, "Is your heart in the right place?" Or in other words, is the real you thinking about this situation in the right way.

We have heard about somebody that has "given their heart away;" that person somehow manages to give all that they are to another person. When we read about or witness how somebody has gotten a broken heart, that person feels as though the center of them is crushed beyond belief. People may languish for years because of a broken heart that has crushed their desire, their will, and their passion in life. It has destroyed their motivation and sometimes their desire to live. It has crushed the deepest part of them.

Passion for anything in life is born in the heart. This is the part of us that gets ignited, that causes us to accomplish anything great. True joy and happiness are birthed from the heart, not from a circumstance or from a roller coaster high. It all comes from the heart.

SO WHAT IS THE HEART?

Webster's Dictionary describes the physical heart as the chambered muscular organ that pumps blood received from the veins into the arteries, thereby maintaining the flow of blood through the entire circulatory system. In many ways our heart of hearts is similar. Everything in our life, every thought we have

Above all else,

guard your heart,

for it is the

wellspring of life.

—PROVERBS 4:23

ever had, every emotion we have ever felt, pumps through the core of our being. Somehow as all that gets pumped through us and we relive emotions, thoughts, and experiences, each of us has a unique heart that begins to shape the directions of our lives and the decisions that we make. Our hearts mold the desires of our lives and lead us places that might or might not be wise. All that we see, hear, and feel are interpreted through our hearts. We absorb these things, and we respond to these things, sometimes without even realizing it. The danger is that no one has taught us to be careful about what we allow into our hearts; we end up absorbing every experience and taking it all into the center of who we are. The heart is really the core of who we are, and it drives our desire. It is very important for us to learn how to make sure only the right things make it into our hearts, so that our hearts don't lead us to a place we regret for the rest of our life.

CHAPTER

POWER OF THE HEART

If you have ever witnessed a space shuttle taking off, you would have seen one of the most dramatic expressions of immediate power known to man. Imagine at the point of takeoff . . . 5 . . . 4 . . . 3 . . . 2 . . . 1 . . . seven million pounds of thrust is generated in a matter of two minutes, taking the shuttle from standing still to roaring about five miles per second until it can maintain its orbit. Space shuttles travel so fast that

THREE

My God, I want to do

what you want.

Your teachings are in

my heart.

—Psalm 40:8 NCV

when a piece of foam flew off and hit one of the wings of the shuttle *Columbia*, it was one of the main causes for the shuttle to disintegrate during its descent. Now that is fast![1]

Just imagine taking one of those jet engines, strapping it to your back, and taking off. It seems kind of absurd, but that is really what we are talking about with the power of the human heart. All that you were born to do, you have the power to do as you tap into your heart. That is why it is so important to make sure you have the right desires in your heart, because whatever you desire will rule in your heart. The power of a driving, passionate heart will take you to wherever that desire tells you to go. In another analogy, whatever you let soak into your sponge, whatever you absorb, the power and the drive in your heart will take you in that direction.

Most people don't even know that they are supposed to screen what they let into their hearts and so their desires go back and forth. One minute they desire to marry one person, the next minute they desire to be with someone they see walking down the street. One minute a person desires to lose weight, and the next minute they desire to eat an ice cream cone. People don't filter what comes into their sponges, so their desires set their courses and their hearts make them feel like they are out of control. That is why people say, "I just can't help it." Well, once you set that desire in your heart it is likely that you can't control it. That is why it is so imperative that we guard what desires we let in there.

God made us with an amazing ability to do things that seem impossible; the power of the human heart defies the odds.

When you play with all your heart, you tap into this inner source of power that thrusts you into doing better than what you think is your best. We have all heard a lot of singers—at a concert, on CD, on television, or at church. Every now and then one sounds distinctly different, as if the singer's heart is soaring out of their mouth while they are

singing. It is the kind of experience that makes you want to run to the singer and ask them, "How did you do that?" It is the kind of singing that makes you feel whatever is burning on the inside of the artist. Many pop icons can sing really well, but very few sing from the depths of their souls. My 13-year-old daughter, Charity, has developed a gift for singing. Some of it has come naturally and she also practices a lot. It's not just the practicing that I hear coming out of her, but I can tell she sings from her heart. I remember the first time she was singing in front of a crowd of thousands of people. In the middle of her song some people began to weep, and

God, my heart is steady.

I will sing and praise

you with all my being.

—Psalm 108:1 NCV

others began to stand, and she was just standing there singing from the depth of her heart.

A power comes from the depth of your heart when you tap into what God has put in there. It moves people, it touches people, and it affects people in ways that no logic can understand. The power of a human heart is unleashed when God touches it in a very specific way.

I am reminded of Jennifer, a young lady who had been broken and hurt so many times that she tried to end her life again and again. She kept going to institutions trying to get better, but every time she was released she would go right back into her depression. She had a horrible home life and finally she was determined to kill herself. She grabbed a knife, went to her bedroom, and turned on the television set. When she turned on the television set she flipped on to an *Acquire the Fire* television program (a program we produce each week that is viewed all around the world). When she flipped through the channels at that moment, she just happened to see me looking right into the camera, looking right at her saying something like, "Maybe you are hurting, you feel like you have no hope and that no one really loves you. Well, God loves you and He wants to wrap His arms around you." At that moment, those words

I pray that Christ will live in your hearts by faith and that your life will be strong in love and be built on love.

—Ephesians 3:17 NCV

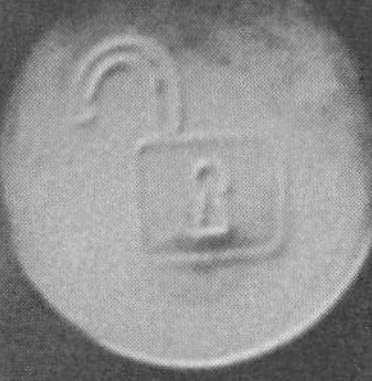

touched her heart so deeply that she put the knife down and gave her heart to the Lord. God lifted the depression off of her, and ever since then she has been a bright example of what can happen in one moment when God touches a human heart.

The power of a human heart to change a total direction of life is untapped by most people. We have all seen these people, the ones that play on a sports team with a half-hearted attitude, go to class with a half-hearted attitude, and acknowledge faith in Christ with a half-hearted attitude. People living out of obligation or just going through motions never tap into the full potential of what God put inside them. Each

and every one of us has the potential to strap on a jet engine and race towards the purpose that God put us here for as we tap into the power of the human heart.

1 Hammer, Eric. NASA Quest. http://quest.arc.nasa.gov. April 10, 1997.

How can a young person
live a pure life?

By obeying your word.

With all my heart I
try to obey you.

Don't let me break
your commands.

I have taken your
words to heart

so I would not sin against you.

—Psalm 119:9–11 NCV

CHAPTER

FUNCTION OF THE HEART

When my two daughters were four and five years old, we began a special ritual when it came to bedtime. This elaborate display of affection began with them building a "throne" on their bed piled high with pillows, blankets, and lace, and them creating a pathway of their best towels, robes, and so forth. As soon as I would walk into the room they would rush across the room, dancing to music and doing their gymnastics flips. They would then escort me to the throne on their "red carpet," seat me on the throne, and then curtsy. Immediately afterward, they would jump on the bed, where with both girls snuggling against my sides, I would read bedtime stories to them. How sad it would have been for them to go through all the work of preparing the room and anticipating our cuddling time only to have me not show up to sit on the throne that was meant for me.

There is a throne like that made by God in each one of our hearts. It is waiting to be filled by the only One it was ever meant for. How sad and frightening it would be for an

Listen, people of Israel! The LORD our God is the only LORD. Love the LORD your God with all your heart, all your soul, and all your strength.

—Deuteronomy 6:4, 5 NCV

imposter to come into my girls' bedroom and force his way onto the throne that was never meant for him—and yet, that is what has happened in the hearts of most humans. We have allowed things to sit on our thrones and essentially rule our desires and destroy our lives. The heart—being the center of our emotions, mind, and will—was always designed to be a holy place, reserved only for the Creator Himself. When working healthily, the function of the physical heart is to keep blood flowing through our bodies, to keep us alive. The function of the emotional heart is to keep us alive, too, to keep life flowing through us, to keep us living passionately—full of life and freedom.

Some people live in a rut. They punch the time clock 8-5 every day, go through the routines of daily life, and perform their chores. They raise their kids and meet their obligations, but they never really live from the heart. They live in drudgery day by day because their heart is not plugged into the Source of life. Even those who play a sport or sing a song with all their heart often experience emptiness when the moment of glory ends. People who have won gold medals or national championships are famous for going into huge bouts of depression; they gave their very best, received the greatest honors, and afterward came up empty because the center of their heart was that gift of sports or performing.

If the LORD doesn't

guard the city,

the guards are

watching for nothing.

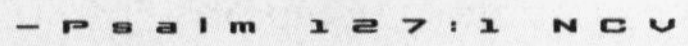

These are the people who end up living with some kind of constant intoxication or mind-numbing drugs, because they have done everything they know to do to pursue their dreams and yet they still feel empty. They are empty because the throne of their heart—designed as a very holy place in their core being—remains empty. They may have accolades, plastic smiles, and the adoration of the world, yet no life.

Living with an empty heart is like a car that is beautiful with a shiny paint job, luxurious interior, and great stereo, but no engine. It's like a computer with a great printer, a big flat screen, the fastest processor, but no hard drive. The world is famous for teaching us how to look like we have everything together on the outside, but if the matters of the heart are not dealt with properly, looking "together" is all an exercise in futility.

Jesus has always wanted to be the object of our desire. That is why in Matthew 6:33 (NKJV), it says, "Seek first the Kingdom of God and His righteousness, and all these things shall be added unto you." In other words, if you are seeking God first, that means that He is your number one desire. If you focus on God by letting Him be your true desire and putting Him on the throne of your life, all the other stuff that the world says is so great, first of all, won't seem so great; and when you have the taste of victory it will be much more fulfilling, because your throne will be occupied by the only Person who was ever meant to be there.

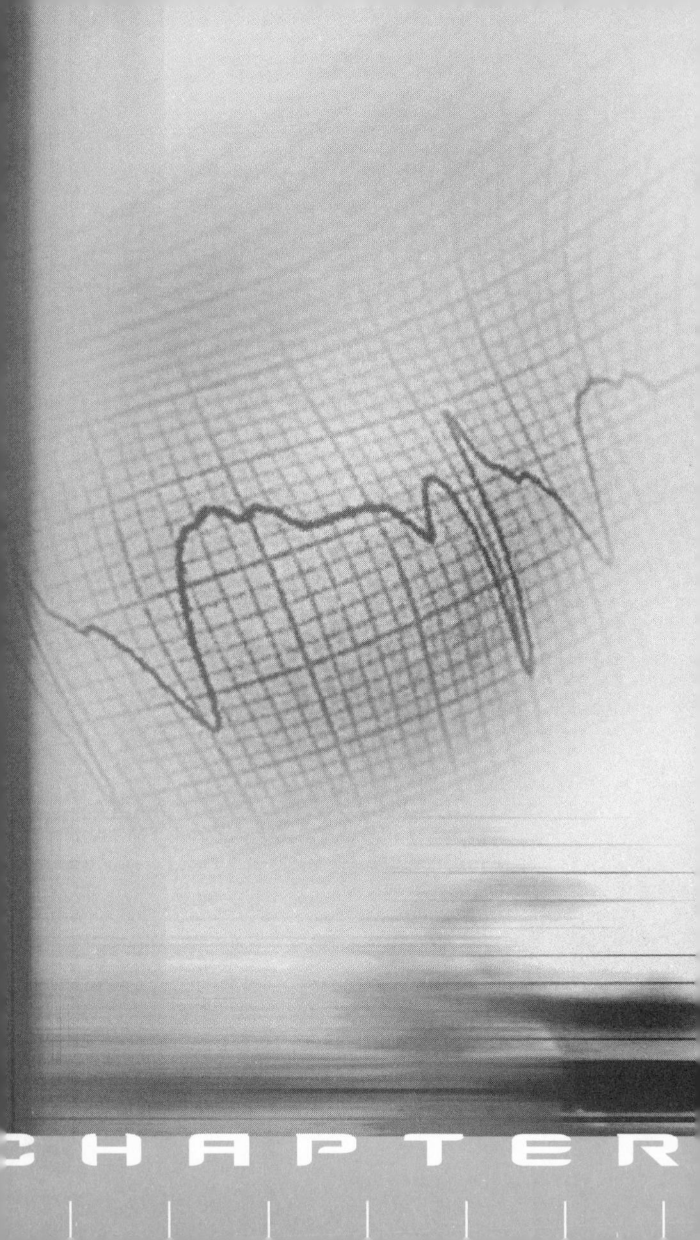
CHAPTER

PRESENT STATE OF THE HEART?

Imagine walking into a doctor's office for a routine checkup. He tells you he detects something that seems abnormal and wants you to go to the hospital for further tests. After being poked and prodded, you are taken to an important-looking room full of very important-looking doctors around a large boardroom table. They tell you the bad news: You have a disease in your heart and unless you have a

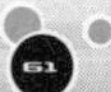

LORD, try me and test me;

look closely into my
heart and mind.

I see your love,

and I live by your truth.

—Psalm 26:2, 3 NCV

heart transplant, you will die within a few months. Shock sets in. It stuns you. You ask if there is any help or any way to control the sickness. They tell you again that there is only one way, one answer, and that is to get a heart transplant. Your mind races with questions about how that could take place. Soon you discover that the heart transplant costs up to $250,000 and you don't have that kind of money or insurance. Then you learn that the list for heart transplants is very long, and you have to start at the bottom of the list. As the terrible news dawns on you, your hopes begin to sink. You realize you could be in the final months of your life on this earth. You ask how you

caught the disease. The doctors tell you that it is inherited; you were born with it. You have had the sickness all along, but just didn't know it, and it is getting worse and worse. Soon you will begin to feel the effects, you will get weaker and weaker, and you will sleep more and more. It will be harder to breathe, and then one day, you just won't wake up. This really is the present state of the human heart.

The Bible says, "Every inclination of [man's] heart is evil from childhood" (Genesis 8:21). God sees right into our hearts and knows that we are born with a disease called sin. Did you ever notice that no one had to teach you how to hit your brother, how to steal his toy, or how to be jealous? We are born with the natural inclination to sin. David said in Psalm 51:5, "Surely I was sinful at birth, sinful from the time my mother conceived me." As a result of our hearts being naturally wicked and evil, Jesus said, our whole lives are affected (Matthew 12:34). The result of having evil hearts born with a disease called sin is that our lifestyles and our attitudes are affected. Jesus said, "For out of the heart comes evil thoughts, murder, sexual immorality, theft, false testimony, and slander, these are what make a man 'unclean'" (Matthew 15:19). In other words, these evil things coming out

of the heart demonstrate the fact that we each have an unclean heart. Furthermore, Jesus said, "[the devil] has blinded their eyes and deadened their hearts, so that they can neither see with their eyes, nor understand with their hearts, nor turn—that I would heal them" (John 12:40).

We are born with a heart disease called sin, and evil comes out of us as a result of that. Sin has blinded our hearts so we can't really see what's right and wrong. We have a world full of evil, hatred, cheating, and lying. We're surrounded by horribly corrupt movies, TV, sitcoms, music, and videos that we absorb just like a sponge soaks up water. We suck all that right into the center of us, compounding the contamination and corruption and turning our inner beings into nothing more than dumps where people unload their garbage. In addition to that, we store many things in our hearts because we don't know where else to put them. For example, maybe you were hurt as a child by some kind of physical or verbal abuse. You don't know what to do with that hurt, or how to process it, so somehow it finds a place in your heart. You end up shutting the door tight and pretending like the pain isn't there. The things that hurt us could be stuff we don't understand, either that happened to us or things we were told, words spoken to us by our parents or even by other kids in school. They told us we were ugly, fat, or stupid, or that we will never amount to anything. Many of those hurtful words are stored in our hearts. Sometimes Bible stories we heard in Sunday school were stored in our hearts, and although we don't understand what significance they had in our life, or what they meant, we hold them in our hearts hoping to make sense out of them. Our hearts have absorbed all that we have seen and heard. The world has made an imprint on us with pornography, music, and materialism. Society and circumstances have hurt us and abused us. We are born into sin with an appetite for more sin. We don't see the effects right away, but eventually, if you look at people without Christ in their lives, they'll begin to exhibit the signs of heart failure.

Remember the heart is the center, the sponge that absorbs everything and the power that drives us. We have been absorbing all these things, so the insults and injuries to our hearts are pushing us to the edge of a cliff. Have you ever seen people who seem to have only bad things happen to them? They keep walking right into trouble and they can't see it? Often it is because the bad things that have been absorbed into their hearts are driving them toward more harm, both physical and spiritual.

After reading this part of the book, you probably feel a lot like the person in the hospital boardroom hearing about the impending heart failure. Such bad news about your heart can push you to the edge of despair, but hang on . . . a miracle is about to happen.

I find rest in God;

only he gives me hope.

He is my rock and
my salvation.

He is my defender;

I will not be defeated.

—Psalm 62:5, 6 NCV

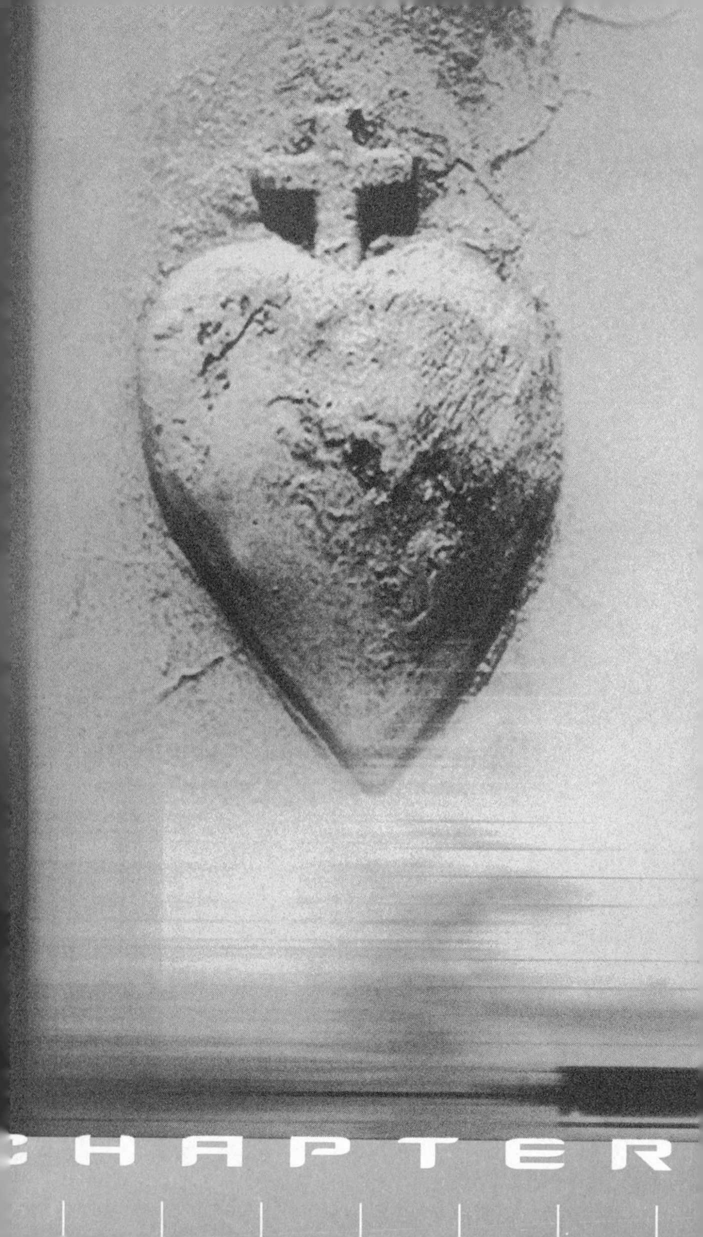
HAPTER

WHAT HAPPENS WHEN GOD CHANGES YOUR HEART?

So there you are, sitting in the hospital, the fact that you have been carrying around this disease for all these years is sinking in, and you're realizing that the illness is about to take its toll on your life. You realize there is basically no chance you are going to get a new heart, when someone strides into the room and offers to pay for a new heart. You can't believe it. Someone would pay that

much to help you? As you wonder about how to survive the long waiting list, your benefactor offers to give his own heart to be transplanted into you, to save your life. You are in shock. You don't know what to say or do. You don't feel worthy. You want to say no to this extreme generosity, but if you do, you will die. How could you accept such a gift? What do you say to that person? How would you say thank you? How could you possibly give him a gift that would be worthy of the gift he is giving you?

This is exactly what Jesus Christ does for us. When we realize that we have a disease in our heart called sin, He offers to pay the price of healing by giving His own life on the

Cross. He donates Himself, so we can get a new heart.

Let's try to understand this new-heart miracle the very best we can with our finite human minds. Ezekiel promises that God will take away our hearts of stone and give us hearts of flesh (Ezekiel 11:19). God also says, "I will put My Spirit within you and cause you to walk in My statutes" (Ezekiel 36:27 NKJV). In other words, He gives each of us a new heart and implants a desire that will make us want to live and walk the way He wants us to live and walk. Desires in our hearts drive us toward what we desire, and God says He will put His own desire in us. What God really wants is our heart. He says

that if we offer Him our diseased hearts, so that He can be the center and sit on the throne, He'll give us new, whole hearts. Our hearts are turned to stone because of the influences we have been talking about: the hardness of sin, the imprint of the world, being born with a sinful nature, and absorbing all the things of the world. All of these things make us hard and cold toward God and others. But He promised to give us a new and tender heart.

What God asks for is clearly laid out in Matthew 22. He asks for it from the very beginning and calls it the most important command. In this chapter, there is a lawyer who is asking about the most important

CHAPTER SIX

"Change your hearts and lives, because the kingdom of heaven is near."

—Matthew 4:17 NCV

rule. Do you ever wonder what the most important command is from that big thick book full of "rules," as the lawyer might have perceived God's Word? If you could boil everything God wants down to one sentence, what do you think it would be? The greatest command is simply this: to love the Lord your God with all your heart, all your soul, all your mind, and all your strength (Matthew 22:37). God really wants our hearts, the deepest parts of us. To give Him our hearts and to have Him be the center of our hearts. To love Him more than all the stuff the world tells us to love. He is asking for the real us, to be the center of all that we are. He wants to be the One who sits on the throne of our lives and who steers where we go. He guides our hearts where He wants to take us once we submit to Him and He comes to live inside us.

Think about it this way: It is so easy for us to say, "I love You, Lord," or to know with our heads that God wants us to love Him with all our hearts, because we have heard it so much in our lives.

Do you realize that of all the religions in the world, Christianity is the only belief system where God is not just a bunch of rules, but He is asking for our hearts? In no other religion does the "god" ask for the heart. Buddha doesn't ask for it, Allah doesn't ask for it, Confucius doesn't ask for

"when they believed,

[God] made their

hearts pure."

—Acts 15:9 NCV

it, and the Hindu gods don't ask for it. All other religions are lists of things to do, supposedly to please their gods, but the Creator, the only true God, along with His Son, Jesus Christ, asks for our hearts because He created our hearts to be thrones occupied only by Him, not by stuff, not by fun, not by adventure, not by entertainment, but by Him. He is the only One who asks for our hearts, and He is also the only One who promises to give us new hearts. No other religion talks about a heart that needs to be changed or even could be changed. Jesus is the only One who promises the miracle of a new heart, and He is the only One who can deliver it.

So how and when does this miracle happen?

The miracle of a new heart happens at the moment of ultimate surrender. Loving the Lord with all your heart seems to be a popular thing today, or at least talking about it is popular. People receive awards for singing perverted songs, and then they thank the Lord. They accept awards for making perverted movies and then thank the Lord for it. People wear Jesus shirts and WWJD bracelets, but then in their lifestyles they do everything the Bible says is wrong. So what does it mean to love the Lord with all your heart? A lot of people talk about God, but very few people love the Lord with all their heart and submit their lives to Him.

We use the word "love" flippantly these days. I love peanut butter and jelly, pizza, your hairstyle, your house, your room, etc. Then, when we say we love the Lord, He is put way up on the list with the cheeseburgers. The love God is talking about is much deeper than that. This is love that comes from the deepest part of our heart. "With all our heart," means from the deepest part of us. It is such a deep love with so much affection that we commit our lives to Him.

If a man was seriously inquiring about marrying a young lady, and he said "I really believe you are the one for me." She would be enamored at first, but if he came back

Now that you have made your souls pure by obeying the truth, you can have true love for your Christian brothers and sisters. So love each other deeply with all your heart.

—1 Peter 1:22 NCV

the next year and said, "I really believe you are the one for me," she would still be excited but a little less enamored. Then if he came back five years later and said the same thing she would get tired and say, "Then you need to commit and give your heart to me." That's the same thing that Jesus asks, "If you really believe I am the One for you, and if you are really going to say that you love Me, then I want you to commit and let Me be the One who is really in charge of your life. I want you to turn away from all the other things that you were following, empty those other things out of your heart and let it be occupied by the only One who was ever meant to live in there."

At that moment—when you turn from the world and you say, "I want all the other stuff out; I am not just going to love the Lord and put Him on the list of all the other stuff I love, but I am going to get rid of all the other stuff in my heart and allow Him to sit where He belongs, as the Boss"—it is at that moment that He breathes life into your dead heart and the miracle of a new heart takes place. The Bible calls it being "born again" (John 3:3). You are born again because you become a brand new person; He gives you a new heart. It is hard to describe with words. You don't have to wonder if your new birth is happening. It is not a cheesy little prayer; it is a commitment of ultimate surrender. It is digging down to the deepest part of you and saying, "Lord, here I am. I am giving myself to You!" At that moment of surrender, He breathes life into a dead heart. He always does it. Sometimes you feel it or you don't; it doesn't matter. A miracle happened! When you take that step, you have just begun to live life as it was really meant to be.

If you have never had the miracle of a new heart happen inside of you, right now is the time to go for it. Right now is the time to pray. Right now, while you are reading this book, right where you are, before you go on to the next chapter, ask Jesus to breathe life into your heart.

Pray this simple prayer, and pray it from depth of your soul. Reach way down deep and let Jesus hear you say these words out loud.

Lord Jesus, I come to You and ask You to forgive me for trying to live my life without You in the very center where You belong. I turn away from the world and all of the things the world has thrown at me, and I come running to You. I believe You died on the cross for me, Jesus, and You rose again. Today, I give You my life and I give You my heart. I wrap my very life and heart around You. I ask You to take the throne and to be the Boss, to be the desire of my heart. I choose to love You with all my heart, my soul, my mind, and my strength. From now on, my life belongs to You, and I will live for You every day for the rest of my life. In Jesus' name, Amen.

The Bible says now God will breathe His life into your heart. As you continue to read this book, you will find out what it means to protect your heart from all the garbage that the world wants to dump on you, so you can live strong in Him for all your days on this earth.

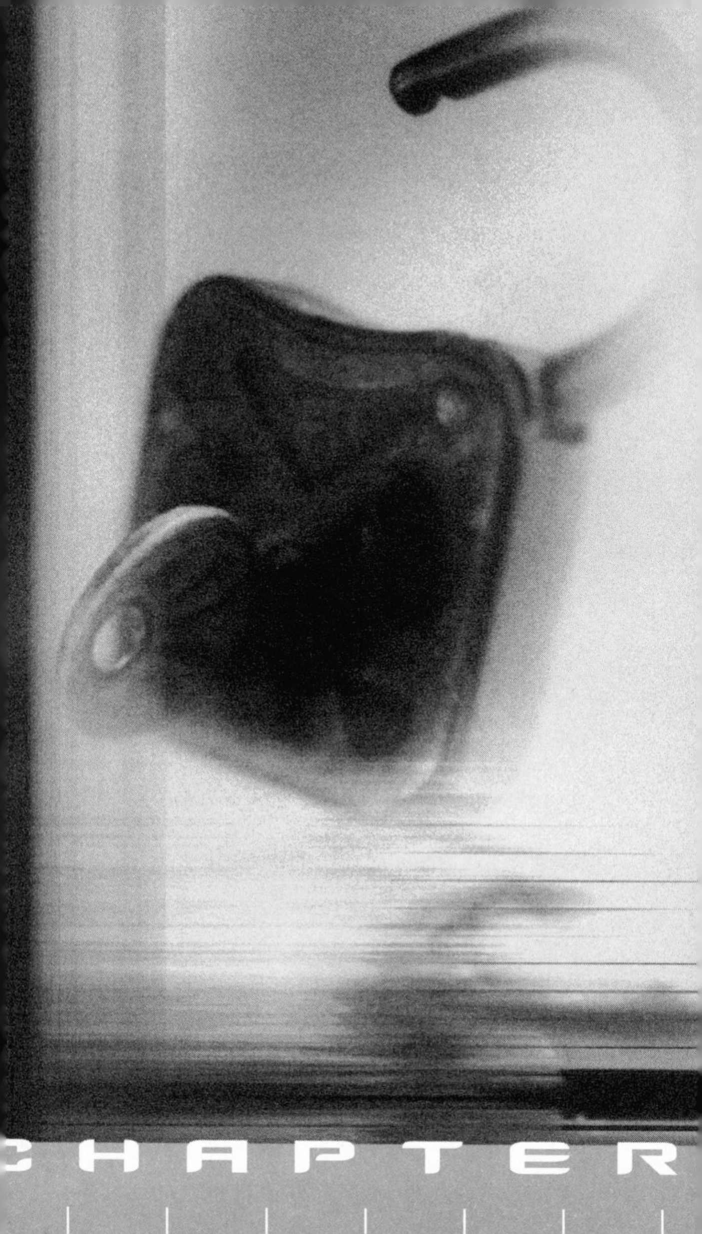
CHAPTER

WHY GUARD YOUR HEART?

"RAINING BLOOD (A CRY FOR HELP)"

A poem by Beth

I'm screaming inside—being torn apart.
But I don't know why—when did this start?
Just sitting here wondering what happened to my heart.

I never thought I could, but now it feels strangely good.
I know it's not right—it just happened one night.
Something sears inside as the emptiness takes flight.

Blood is raining, my soul is straining,
And I cannot contain all this horrible pain,
It takes everything I've got just to get through the day.
The numbness burns, and they cannot know.
I don't need their concern; I can't let the pain show.

They all surround me and yet I'm terribly alone.
I'm caught up in the chains of the mystical pain.
I don't want to die; I want only to fly.
I just can't figure out what's making me cry.
Blood is raining, my dreams are fading,
And all this pain cannot be restrained.

I'm tired of waiting for all the somedays.
Who will teach me to smile again?
I just need someone to be my friend,
Someone to shelter me from this pain,
Just to help me through these days;
Won't someone please try to make things okay?

I just don't know what's making me sad,
They tell me I've never seen strife,
So explain to me why it hurts so bad.
They say I have a great life,
They obviously don't know about the hypnotic knife.

Blood is raining, softly serenading,
Overwhelmed by shame, giving into the pain,
Won't someone please end this sickening game?

These are the words of a thirteen-year-old girl named Beth. Think about the impact of these words. Here is a young lady who supposedly has it all together, but Beth is hurting so badly on the inside of her heart that she tries to distract herself from the pain by cutting herself again and again. This is just one of the many kinds of horrible tragedies that happen when we don't guard our hearts. We listen to lies and we get infected with the confusion of the world. It manipulates our emotions, causing us to despair and get depressed. We end up becoming products of our environment. The Bible says, "My people are destroyed from lack of knowledge" (Hosea 4:6). Even many of God's people—who have new hearts and have Jesus living inside of them—die or are destroyed because they

don't know how He wants them to live, nor do they know that each of us must guard our heart, protect it, and take care of it. They don't know that we all must guard our hearts with His Word because out of the heart comes the wellspring of life (Proverbs 4:23). In other words, guarding our hearts is essential to all of life.

Your heart is meant to be a wellspring of life; it's meant to bring you joy, passion, and a thriving appreciation for all that is holy, righteous, and pure. If you don't guard it, and you allow in all the stuff that we have been talking about, you will end up paying a price, even if you call yourself a Christian. As I speak to young people each weekend all across America, I see thousands

LORD, help me control
my tongue;

help me be careful
about what I say.

Take away my desire
to do evil

or to join others
in doing wrong.

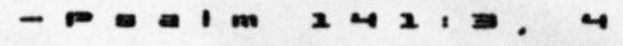

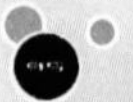

of examples of young people who have not guarded their hearts because no one ever taught them to. They are broken, hurting, and confused. Just a few weeks ago, a seventeen-year-old girl walked up to me, sobbing and saying, "I just want to die, I just want to die, I just want to die." Why guard your heart? Because destruction is the fruit of those who don't know that they should. This is the desire of the enemy of our soul, to make us want to just give up and throw in the towel.

IF WE DON'T GUARD OUR HEARTS WE END UP . . .

:: BROKEN-HEARTED

We end up with our very centers crushed because we let others into our hearts. We opened up our heart to somebody, began to trust them, and then they violated that trust. This is what happens when a husband and wife get divorced. They trusted each other with their hearts and committed "until death do us part," and then the trust was broken. When we don't guard our hearts in our romantic relationships, even if we're just dating casually, the same thing can happen. The average person dates and gets their heart broken

ten times before they get married; that's a lot of brokenness. We say it is a normal part of growing up, but it doesn't have to be. In God's mind, He doesn't want anybody's heart to be broken. He wants to protect each heart. The way we protect our hearts is not to give them away to anyone but God.

:: HARD-HEARTED

We think that we always know what is right and no one else does, and we don't want to hear what they have to say.

:: COLD-HEARTED

We are afraid to let people come near us, emotionally. We feel like everybody is out to get us and to hurt us, so we push them away.

Lot was a good man, but because he lived with evil people every day, his good heart was hurt by the evil things he saw and heard.

—2 Peter 2:8 NCV

:: FAINT-HEARTED/DEPRESSED

:: HAVING A WOUNDED HEART

We trusted somebody, maybe a family member or a friend, who let us down or somehow someone stabbed us in the back. We walk around with those injuries like a black cloud over our lives. Unforgiveness begins to fester inside of us like a cancer getting worse and worse, turning into anger, then bitterness, then rage. Even if we are in the right and the other people are in the wrong, we end up damaged, maybe even emotionally crippled. Psychologists and psychiatrists see ailments every day that are supposedly "normal" in our society, but in fact the problems are brought on because people have not guarded their hearts. People hurt for years, sometimes spending their whole lives cold, lonely, and depressed. Like the teenage girl I mentioned, they just want to die. But they don't have to hurt that way because Jesus gives us hope: "Do not let your hearts be troubled and do not be afraid." (John 14:27). In other words, He is saying, "You don't have to let your heart be troubled. You don't have to live like this or let the world dictate the state of your heart, your attitude, and your choices."

The great news is that when Jesus gives us our new hearts, He also can take the brokenness and the circumstances that have crushed us on the inside and put us back together. Jesus said He came to heal the broken-hearted (Luke 4:18), to take all the pieces of each broken heart and put them back together. He came to put broken lives back together. So many people have wept out of bitter loneliness for years with so much pain that they feel like there is no way it could ever be taken away. They drink, they get rebellious, they join clubs, gangs, and cliques—all the while still hurting. They inflict violence or hurt on other people trying to distract from their pain, but that doesn't make it go away. No drug, no alcohol, and no prescribed medicine can take away the brokenness. There is only one way—only Jesus can heal the brokenness of our lives.

How does this healing happen? We bring our brokenness to Him and let Him begin a deep healing process. For many of us, the brokenness starts when we are very young. My parents got divorced when I was seven years old, and because of things said and done to me my whole life, I felt like I was nothing. I thought I would never do anything or accomplish anything. The cruel words spoken to me by my parents were only compounded by the cruel actions of the kids at school. I remember wanting to end my own life. I remember hurting so bad on the inside, not having any idea of what I could do to end that pain. This is what happens when we don't guard our hearts. Finally, soon after I committed my life to

You were taught to be

made new in your hearts,

to become a new person.

That new person is made

to be like God—made to

be truly good and holy.

—Ephesians 4:23, 24 NCV

Jesus at sixteen years old, I took all my brokenness, the hurt feelings, and painful memories from a crushed and shattered childhood, and crying a river of tears, I brought all those memories to Him. He began to wash my mind with forgiveness and wash my heart with understanding of how I didn't have to live in that bitterness and pain for the rest of my life. I understand what the Bible means when it says, "If the Son sets you free, you will be free indeed" (John 8:36), because I am really free of all the brokenness that happened to me. You can be free, too, if you bring your brokenness to Him right now. He will bind up your broken heart.

CHAPTER

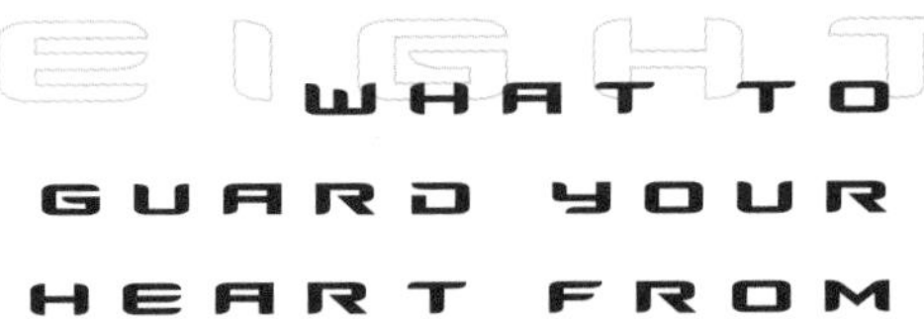

Eight: What to Guard Your Heart From

NORAD (North American Aerospace Defense Command) is a military organization that is designed to protect the United States and Canada from attack. This international partnership has sophisticated radars, satellites, and intelligence systems that enable the armed forces to detect danger coming from anywhere in the world. After

September 11, 2001, instead of just focusing on danger coming from outside, NORAD also began monitoring potential threats from within the borders of the United States and Canada.

We need to be like a spiritual NORAD for our hearts. We must be on the lookout for all the enemy's tricks and tactics that will try to destroy our hearts and our lives. We love God, and we put Him at the centers of our lives. But if we let the enemy destroy our hearts, infect our emotions, and deceive us, we still might make it to heaven, but we'll have a pretty miserable time here on earth. Let's look at the tactics that the enemy uses to invade us, so we can begin to guard against his lies.

MEDIA:

We all must guard our hearts from the media. Some of the enemy's most clever tactics involve invading our hearts through what we watch and what we hear. Something seems cool, funny, or popular. It's got a good groove so we listen to it, we watch it, and we soak it all up. The enemy uses the media to paint false pictures in our minds of what God is like, what's acceptable behavior, what love is like, what relationships are like, all in the name of being cool. Media outlets do it because of money; we do it because we want to be entertained. We have to guard our hearts and our minds from letting the out-of-whack world tell us

what normal life should be like. There is a statistic floating around that says something like 98% of all people are shaped by media. If you don't believe it, just look around and take your own poll. People plan their lives by what's on TV on which night. They can't wait until the next CD of their favorite band comes out or when the next tour of that group is coming to their city. People are consumed with the next movies that are coming out. Their lives revolve around the media's offerings, and then they are further shaped by the programs they watch and music they hear. Many Christians know more lines from movies than from Scripture, and more lyrics from secular songs than from hymns. No wonder they

Guard what God has trusted to you. Stay away from foolish, useless talk and from the arguments of what is falsely called "knowledge." By saying they have that "knowledge," some have missed the true faith. Grace be with you.

—1 Timothy 6:20, 21 NCV

blame God when they are hurting. They think they have committed themselves to the Lord, so how could He allow hurtful things to happen? Well, it is really not God who allowed the pain to happen, but it was they themselves who asked for it by inviting the garbage of the world into their lives; even though they call themselves Christians, their hearts and their lives are still being predominately shaped by the media, not by Scripture.

DECEPTION:

We have to guard our hearts against deception. The enemy knows that we won't follow him if he openly walks up to us with a pitchfork and two big horns, so he has become a master deceiver. He deceives us in all forms. He masquerades as an "angel of light" (2 Corinthians 11:14). He looks innocent, he looks fun, he looks cool, all the while, putting rings in our noses and pulling us down. We have got to be on the lookout for him, and we do that by studying the Word ourselves so we can see what truth really is. That way, when Liar comes walking along, asking us to join him, we can uncover the deceptive plot instead of falling for it.

Let everyone see that

you are gentle and kind.

The Lord is coming

soon. Do not worry

about anything, but

pray and ask God for

everything you need,

always giving thanks.

And God's peace, which

is so great we cannot

understand it, will keep

your hearts and minds

in Christ Jesus.

Brothers and sisters,

think about the things

that are good and

worthy of praise.

Think about the things

that are true and

honorable and right

and pure and beautiful

and respected. . . . And

the God who gives

peace will be with you.

—Philippians 4:5–9 NCV

BITTERNESS:

So many circumstances can provoke bitterness. Somebody could do something to us that could be genuinely wrong. We get angry, then furious, then we fly into a rage, and after we have been in a rage for a while, it becomes a bitter root. Even though we say we love God, this bitterness could cause us to live with poison on the inside of us, cause us to age prematurely, cause our bones to rot, and ultimately destroy the quality of life that Jesus died to give us. We all must guard our hearts from bitterness. If we have been angry, if we have been hurt, even if we have a right to be mad, we need to turn it over to the Lord, ask God to forgive us for being angry, and ask Him for the power to forgive others. Letting it go is our decision, not the devil's. We have to guard our hearts from bitterness by giving up our unforgiveness and asking the Lord to take it off our shoulders and out of our hearts.

BEING LURED AND ENTICED INTO SIN:

James 1:14 says that each man is led into sin when he is enticed by the world. The world is constantly trying to lure us: "Just buy this. Just try this. Just get drunk this one time. Just have sex this one time." Even well-meaning friends, who might even call themselves Christians, sometimes say, "Do you think you are going to go to hell if you do it just this one time?" The lures look so attractive. People use circular logic that makes you feel like an idiot if you don't give in. "You're a prude. You are close-minded. Don't you realize that we live in the twenty-first century?" We have to be wise, because the lure will put us right where it has put millions of others. It will throw us right into slavery that will wreck our lives. Many times it is that one time of getting drunk that will cause a catastrophe to happen. Maybe that one time involved in sex could get somebody pregnant or sick with a disease. There is always a price to pay for sin, and we have got to be able to see through the temptations and guard our hearts from being lured. Instead of going as close as we can to the edge of the cliff of sin without actually falling off it, we need to stay as far back from the cliff as we possibly can, and refuse to be enticed to its edge.

HURT:

We need to guard our hearts against hurt. Let me show you a glimpse of an e-mail we recently received. We get so many e-mails like this from young people from across America.

> *"I get so upset and angry I want to die. I don't understand why God is not offering a little help. On top of*

that, my parents want me to move to a whole different state where we know no one, so even if I sneak a call or visit, who would it be? Why is God not here to stop me from hurting myself, or hurting so bad? Why am I wandering so far away? Why would God not help me get just some light in my world and a little hope and a little better life, a little grace? JUST LET ME STOP HURTING FROM INSIDE AND OUT!"

—lost friend in life

Circumstances surround this young woman, obviously, beyond what she can control. We can't control a lot of things that happen to us, but we can control how we react to them. We have to guard our hearts against living as victims because of what has happened to us. The brokenness that has tormented our souls needs to be brought to the Lord, and He will give us the grace and help we need to deal with it. He will rally others around us to stand with us as well. We need to see the incoming enemies of our souls trying to get to our centers and inflict hurt that will keep us broken our whole lives. We need to submit our hurt to God so that it doesn't take root in us and destroy us.

RELATIONSHIPS:

We need to guard our hearts from relationships. I mentioned earlier that it's

A happy heart is like

good medicine,

but a broken spirit

drains your strength.

—Proverbs 17:22 NCV

common for people to get broken hearts because we just give our hearts away so often and so casually. Our society tells us that if you don't have a boyfriend or girlfriend all the time that you are weird, stupid, fat, and ugly, and that you don't really belong. All of that is a lie from hell. The enemy promotes a perverted sense of love, and so people don't know where real love comes from. They don't know God's big-time love, and so they do their best to fill themselves with some kind of imitation love. We have to be smart enough to see through the lies. Instead of chomping at the bit and complaining, "Mom, why can't I date until I am sixteen?" we have to be smarter than other people and realize that it is a

huge distraction to get emotionally involved with someone you are probably not going to marry. Falling "in love" too soon means you'll probably get your heart crushed, and in the process, give away your purity. So many people who never intended to throw away their purity end up losing it because they gave their heart away first. You have to be smarter than that and see the incoming weaponry of a bright-eyed guy or girl and realize they could be the biggest distraction of your life. People say, "It's just a part of growing up. It is just a part of what everybody goes through." No, it is a part of growing up in a worldly way, the way the world says is normal. But broken hearts and giving purity away are "normal," too. We don't need to be a part of what the world says is normal.

ACTING ON WHIMS:

We need to guard our hearts from acting on whims. This covers a lot of different circumstances. We feel "led" this way, or we impulsively go that way, and we get ourselves in all kinds of trouble instead of guiding our lives and our decisions based on really thinking about what Jesus would do. If Jesus really is the center of our life, then what does His Word say about how we should be living? We should always be guarding our hearts, even when we're with our Christian friends. How many times have

we done something and we think, "Why did I do that . . . that was stupid, stupid, stupid!" Well, it is time to be smart now. If the enemy can get us to do something without really thinking about it, we'll be falling in pothole after pothole. We have to guard ourselves against whims.

These are just a few things to guard ourselves from. It comes down to the fact that we ought to be surveying the land all the time, and if the things that are trying to invade our hearts don't line up with God's Word, we ought to deny them entrance to our minds, our hearts, and ultimately our lives.

Obey my commands,

and you will live.

Guard my teachings as you

would your own eyes.

Remind yourself of them;

write them on your heart

as if on a tablet.

—Proverbs 7:2, 3 NCV

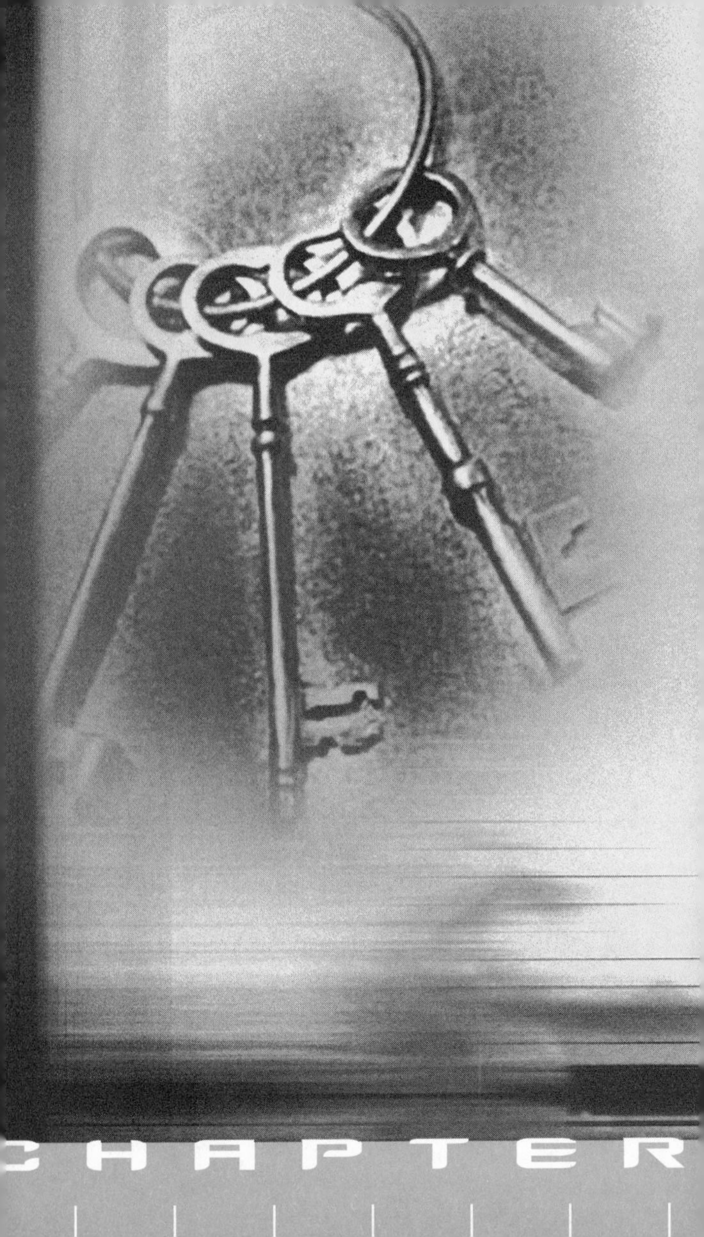
CHAPTER

NINE

HOW TO GUARD YOUR HEART

As you are reading this, whatever you do, do not think about little pink monkeys. Whatever you do, DO NOT think about little pink monkeys. Quit picturing their arms and their legs, don't think about them climbing trees and swinging around. Whatever you do, don't think about little pink monkeys. The problem is, every time you read "little pink monkeys" those little monkeys fly through your mind. Similarly, when we talk

about guarding our hearts, we have to talk about more than just what not to do. "Don't think about the hurt, don't think about the pain, and don't think about the media . . ." Whatever you think about or look at endears you to that thing. I mentioned James 1:14 in the last chapter where he cautions against being enticed by the world. The world lures us by getting us to look at it long enough that we get distracted from what God wants and drawn in by what the enemy wants. Looking at the things that tempt us feeds the evil, sinful nature lurking in us. The more we look at temptation, the more we say, "Well, I am not really doing it, I am just being tempted. The more we ponder a temptation, the more it entices, fuels, and energizes us. Remember, our hearts are like sponges. They absorb what we expose them to. The longer we stare at those advertisements or websites, the more we want what they're selling instead of what God has given.

Think about the last time you saw a really great trailer for a movie. You wanted to see it so badly. You couldn't stop thinking about the images and when it was going to come out into theaters. And then as soon as it was released, you went to see it. What happened? You saw a little bit of it, and it enticed you and won you. You may be thinking, "Well, that wasn't the devil; a movie wouldn't hurt me." Well, I'm talking about something bigger than one movie. The more you stare at the world, the more

it fuels your heart with desire for the world. Some of us get so mad at ourselves because we try to follow God, but we keep falling away. We keep falling away because we stare at temptations long enough for them to fuel our desires. Temptations put those desires in our hearts until finally it's like a car running off the edge of a cliff because the driver got distracted. In the same way, when we get distracted from Jesus long enough, we throw our lives over the cliff.

So, what's the cure? Colossians 3:2 talks about it. "Set your minds on things above, not on earthly things." We must choose to set our hearts and minds in the right direction. Godly stuff will not accidentally

Put out of your life every evil thing and every kind of wrong. Then in gentleness accept God's teaching that is planted in your hearts, which can save you.

—James 1:21 NCV

fly through our brains. Holy stuff will not be the natural course of our every thought. Why? Because our sinful nature wants to keep dominating us, but we don't have to let it be the boss. The Bible says that we have to set our hearts. In other words, we have to focus our hearts, our attentions, and our affections on whatever is true, holy and righteous; on the things above; and on the things of the Bible. The more we set our minds, the more desire we will have to go in the right direction. As our good desires build, they will thrust our lives with the rocket power of the Holy Spirit in the direction of God.

We guard our hearts by setting our minds and hearts on the things above.

Think about the concept of setting your mind. You don't let just anything enter your mind; you set it on Him. You don't let just anything come into your ears; you choose what you listen to. You don't just let your eyes stare at whatever they happen to see; you choose to keep your eyes on what is holy, godly, and righteous, and you close them when there is ungodliness around. You choose as your best friends the people who are really going to love God. The psalmist said that the more we set our minds and hearts on Him, the more we'll long for Him like we desire water in a dry and weary land (Psalm 63); like the deer in Psalm 42 that pants for water, our souls will long after Him.

God protects me like a shield;

He saves those whose

hearts are right.

—Psalm 7:10 NCV

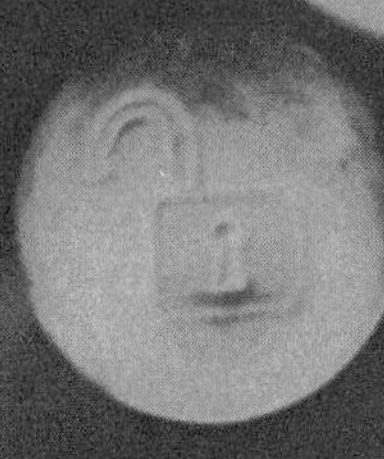

God is looking for a generation of people who will truly long after Him from the very depths of their hearts. A powerful generation that will focus on Him and set their minds and their hearts on Him long enough that He truly becomes the object of their affections; that He is not just another thing on the list . . . "I like my car, my room, I like my clothes, and oh, I like You, Jesus." A generation that holds Him as the Holy Affection of the deepest part. After all, that is what the deepest part in each of us, the heart, was meant to do. Not just to know Him, but to desire, long, and yearn for His greatness to be known in the deepest part of us. He is waiting for us to set our eyes on Him and to gaze at Him. The more we gaze at Him, the more He fuels our hearts to love Him more. The more we gaze at Him, the more we are stunned at His greatness.

We don't have to strive to be a Christian, to try to do good things. Just look at Jesus and He'll draw you like a magnet. He'll entice you towards godliness. Have you ever gone grocery shopping when you were really hungry, so you end up with way more stuff than you wanted? Have you ever gone to a restaurant when you were really hungry, so you ordered more than you could eat? You were enticed by that stuff. What if we came to church like that? Saying, "Oh Lord, I want to get some holiness and some purity and some grace today. I want to learn Your Word." It is like you are going through the mall picking up everything you ever wanted. You are going through the Bible and walking down the Hall of Holiness packing everything you can into your life. What if you went to youth group every week and into your quiet time every morning saying, "Okay, Lord, I am hungry," and your eyes get bigger than your heart. "Lord, feed me this morning," as you set your mind and heart on Him, so that He will fuel your desire for Him.

This was the life that we were meant to live. Life from a heart that has been set free, a heart that has been renewed, and a heart that is fueled by desire for Him because we choose to set our mind and heart on Him. This is the life of freedom that He desires

LORD, teach me what you
want me to do,

and I will live by your truth.

Teach me to respect
you completely.

Lord, my God, I will praise
you with all my heart,

and I will honor
your name forever.

—Psalm 86:11, 12

for every human being. First of all, to be set free from sin, but then to be set free from every care and every anxiety of the world, so that nothing has a hold on us. We walk in joy, we walk in freedom, and we walk in peace because He is our life. He has truly become the object of our affection. We have been swept off our feet by the God of the Universe who loves us so much that He gave His Son's life for us.

When someone loves you that much, don't they deserve all of your heart?

Inside me is a place called Desire. My desires ultimately govern what I do with my body, my mind, and my time. Right now in my life I desire: ______________________

I want to truly desire ______________________

My heart is the wellspring of my life. It is the sponge that soaks up everything I experience and tries to make emotional sense of it all. Some of the things I have let soak into my heart are: ______

______

______

______

______

Some of the changes I want to make in what I soak into my heart are: ______

______

______

______

______

______

______

My heart is a jet engine that rockets me wherever I choose to go. When I unleash this power, I feel

The amazing power of my heart has helped me

There's a throne in my heart. ____________ sits on that throne. When God sits on the throne everything is much more fulfilling and purposeful. When He's not on the throne, things fall apart. Here's how I'm taking care of the Royal Throneroom and the One who's supposed to preside there.

I was born with a fatal heart disease called "sin." The sins I struggle with the most are:

Jesus promised to heal me from my sin. He'll give me a new heart. His heart! Here's how I know that my heart condition is not hopeless and that I'll be okay.

My heart has been hurt, over and over again. Sometimes I've felt: broken-hearted, hard-hearted, cold-hearted, depressed, betrayed. But Jesus can heal my brokenness. Drugs, alcohol, sex, sensory overload—those things only mask my pain—but Jesus can actually heal me. If I let Him. Here's what I'm willing to let Jesus do in my life.

149

It's a dangerous world for me and my heart. I have to guard my heart when dealing with things like media, deception, bitterness, temptation, hurt, whims, and even relationships. But when I'm aware of the dangers, I stand a better chance of protecting my inner treasure. Here are the specific things that most threaten my heart.

No matter how hard I concentrate on what I'm protecting my heart FROM, it'll never work unless I concentrate even more on what I'm protecting my heart FOR. Instead of constantly thinking about bad things, I need to focus my mind on good things. I need to look up, not down. And I need to choose friends who do the same. God wants me to be powerful from the depth of my heart and to truly desire Him. When I look up at Him, here's what I see of myself as reflected in His eyes.

Here's what I want to see.

ACKNOWLEDGEMENTS

Nothing gets done by itself. All good things are done with the help of others. The author wishes to thank Francie Harrell and Kristin Jessee for typing this manuscript, and Juliana Diaz for editing it.

ABOUT THE AUTHOR

President and Founder Ron Luce started Teen Mania Ministries with his wife, Katie, in 1986. He has traveled to more than fifty countries proclaiming the gospel of Jesus Christ. His dream is to empower young people to stand up for Christ in their schools and in the world. Ron meets with thousands of teenagers every week and would love to meet with you when he comes to your city. Call 1-800-299-TEEN (8336) or check out www.TeenMania.com to get in touch with him or learn more.

:: TEEN MANIA MINISTRIES is all about helping young people realize the power of the One who made them and the power of the one He made them to be. Here's what we do:

:: TEEN MANIA GLOBAL EXPEDITIONS. Thousands of young people are changing the world as they travel around the globe on mission trips every year.

:: ACQUIRE THE FIRE YOUTH CONVENTIONS. Teen Mania hosts weekly youth conventions across North America where teens learn how to live in passionate pursuit of Christ.

:: ACQUIRETHEFIRE.COM. Over nine million people visit our website each month to surf our devotions, chat rooms, and discussion boards.

:: ACQUIRE THE FIRE DOME EVENTS. Over the past several years, Teen Mania has hosted a dome event that annually challenges 50,000-70,000 teens in their faith.

:: ACQUIRE THE FIRE TV SHOW. Ron Luce is the host of a weekly program for teens that airs on several television outlets, such as the Trinity Broadcasting Network and Daystar.

:: TEEN MANIA HONOR ACADEMY. Each year, high school graduates live on the Teen Mania campus in Garden Valley, Texas, for an exciting one-year program that emphasizes faith, leadership, purpose, vision, integrity, and honor.

:: EXTREME CAMPS. No other summer camp compares! Bands, speakers, intense spiritual growth, and the most fun imaginable combined into one week.

Run away from the evil young people like to do. Try hard to live right and to have faith, love, and peace, together with those who trust in the Lord from pure hearts.

—2 Timothy 2:22 NCV